People Who Look Like Me

By: Alexis Jackson

People Who Look Like Me

Copyright © 2020 Alexis Jackson

All rights reserved. This book is protected by copyright laws of the United States of America. This book may not be copied or reprinted for commercial gain or profit.

Published by:

Relentless Publishing House, LLC

www.relentlesspublishing.com

Printed in USA
First Printing: March 2020

ISBN: 978-1-948829-32-8

People Who Look Like Me

1 in 20 people have a disability. That gives 19 kids a daily opportunity to learn about diversity, collaboration, inclusion, and friendship.

~Unknown

Hello! My name is Alex. I am 7 years old and I have autism. I am not too sure what having autism means, but I will try to explain.

Autism Spectrum Disorder impacts my nervous system, which tends to slows down my development and interferes with my interaction with others, but I feel fine. I just wish the kids at school would see me the same way.

Having autism causes others to treat me like I am a little baby, as if I am not capable of doing anything on my own.

In class every morning I come to school with my book bag prepared for class, ready to answer all the questions because I am one smart cookie!

But no one calls on me to help them answer any of the mathematical questions, I yell and squirm and say, "Pick me, pick me," but no one seems to call on me.

When gearing up for recess, I bring out my favorite shoes that gives me the speed as fast as lightning in hopes that someone will include me in the fun.

I run down the field screaming, "I am open, I am open," hoping someone will pass me the football, but everyone continues to throw in the opposite direction.

I even try to race the fastest kid in my class and let me tell you, he is fast! And he even turns down my offer. He never turns down a competition.

I often kick and scream because no one treats me like the other kids and it causes me to cry. I know it may frighten others but I just want to be treated the same.

Having autism does not mean I cannot solve that math problem in class.

Play catch with the ball during recess.

Or even race the fastest kid in my class.

Having autism just means I develop the skill to interact and learn a little slower than the others, but I am still capable of doing the same things any other kid can do. All I need is a little encouragement and for kids to embrace people who look like me.

God created me a little different but are we not all different in our own unique ways?

www.ingramcontent.com/pod-product-compliance
Lightning Source LLC
Chambersburg PA
CBHW041722040426
42451CB00003B/23